Gary Jones

Madrid

First published by Gary Jones in 2016.

Copyright © Gary Jones, 2016.

All rights reserved. No part of this publication may be reproduced, stored, or transmitted in any form or by any means, electronic, mechanical, photocopying, recording, scanning, or otherwise without written permission from the publisher. It is illegal to copy this book, post it to a website, or distribute it by any others means without permission.

This book was professionally typeset on Reedsy.
Find out more at reedsy.com

Contents

Introduction	1
Weather And The Best Time To Visit	4
Background And History	7
Transport In Madrid	10
Hotels	19
Museums	23
Art Galleries	29
Shopping In Madrid	33
Dining In Madrid	36
Bars And Nightlife	41
Special Things To Do While In Madrid	48
Three Day Sample Itinerary	53
Conclusion	59

1

Introduction

What comes to mind at the thought or mention of Madrid? Well, different things will probably cross different people's minds but one of the common ones will be Real Madrid Football Club, the fun people and Spanish bullfighting just to mention a few but there is more to Madrid than just that.

With a city population of over 3.3 million and a metro area that prides in over 6.5million residents coupled with the fact that it prides in its artistic and cultural heritage and a people that never sleeps, you can bet that there is a lot you can experience. Madrid is the largest city in Spain and dates back to the 2nd century BC when the Roman Empire established a settlement at the banks of Manzanares River then named it Matrice.

Over the years, the city has grown to become the headquarters of World Trade Organization (WTO), the residence of the Spanish Monarch, the seat of the government of Spain and the economic, political, and cultural center of Spain. Its urban agglomeration has the EU's third largest GDP and has been ranked the world's 17th most livable city in the world by Monocle magazine in its 2014 index.

Besides Real Madrid FC, Atlético de Madrid is also another football club with base in Madrid. Currently, Madrid has 21 districts, which have been further divided into 128 wards (also known as barrios)-the picture below shows the 21 districts. If you are planning to visit Madrid, make this book your guide as it will help you uncover many of the places you'd probably not want to miss.

I hope you enjoy your trip!

2

Weather And The Best Time To Visit

The best time of the year to travel to Madrid is probably Spring and Autumn. The air is crisp and the weather mild, but the two seasons feature some differences that you may want to account for when planning a trip to the city.

Spring runs from March to May, and days are warm, while the nights are cool. People flood into the streets for the trendy "marcha" where people walk across the city, step into bars, chat on the streets, and simply have fun outdoors. Holy Week is a particularly good time to visit the city, when the residents leave the city for vacation. There are some wind and some rain, but it is generally okay.

Autumn, which runs from September, all through November, is the time schools are opened, and people get back to work after the August holidays. This is usually marked with plenty of cultural activities. Compared to the high temperatures in August, the days are very pleasant.

During winter, which runs from December to March, the number of tourists is not so much, and it can be a good time to travel, if you don't mind some cold and some snow. Since this is a low tourist season, you will enjoy great bargains at trips and hotels around Madrid.

The feared summer that runs from June, all through August is not as bad as it is publicized. The momentum is kind in June, harsh in July and harsher in August. Nights in June are long and warm, and you can really take pleasure in the party atmosphere in the streets. July is marked with temperatures hitting over 40 Degrees Celsius, and does not cool down that much during the night.

3

Background And History

Madrid, originally known as Mayrit, was established at the end of the 9th century by the emir Muhammad. The city gained relevance under the Arab inhabitation of the Iberian Peninsula, given that Toledo had been the major city in the Spanish plain.

During the Christian re-conquest of Spain, Madrid changed hands from Muslims to Christians several times, leading to the mixture of cultures that features the city to date. The current location of Madrid, at the heart of Spain, was founded in 1083 by King Alfonso I. Under Christian rule, all Muslim symbols were eliminated from the city and part of the city's cultural heritage was lost.

In the course of the next centuries, Madrid developed to reach its current aspect. Plaza Mayor (The Main Square) was founded in the 13th century under the auspice of John II. Enrique III later ordered the building of El Pardo into a dwelling place for royal visits. Madrid kept growing in size, and the Spanish Court was finally transferred to the city from its current location in Toledo. It was moved again in 1601 to Valladolid, before being definitively returned to Madrid five years later.

The nineteenth century was a gloomy time for Madrid, following bloody historical events like the rise of the city against French dominance on 2nd May 1808, as well as the onset of the Spanish War of Independence.

After the death of General Franco in the 20th century, the 1978 Spanish Constitution affirmed Madrid as Spain's capital city.

The first democratic elections were held in 1979 in the city to elect the first city mayor. Enrique Tierno Galvan was voted the first governor of Madrid. By this time, the city had grown in size and population to reach a figure of three million people in the metropolitan area, and almost six million inhabitants in the entire province of Madrid.

4

Transport In Madrid

Getting In

Before you can start moving around the city, you need to get to it first. Let's take a quick look at the transport options on how to get into Madrid.

By Plane

Adolfo Suárez Madrid-Barajas Airport (IATA: MAD, is the main international airport, and one of the largest in Europe. It is located about 13km from the city center.

Adolfo Suárez Madrid-Barajas Airport Website
http://www.aeropuertomadrid-barajas.com/eng/
Adolfo Suárez Madrid-Barajas Airport MAP
https://goo.gl/maps/NeFVg8nZYyG2
Phone:+34 913 21 10 00

When you get here, you can use the express bus services usually available 24 hours and passes all the 4 terminals then goes to O'Donell, Cibeles, which is around a 20 minutes walk or a pretty fast metro ride to Puera del Sol and Atocha. You will incur about €5, paid to the driver; there is a bus after 12 minutes during the day and every 35minutes during the night.

If you don't want to use the bus, use the metro (this is line 8pink starting from 06.30 to 01.30) to Nuevos Ministerios station. Please note that you will change the line twice if you use this option.

You can also use the public bus 200, which moves from the airport to Avenida de America bus station in Madrid. This will cost about 1.5 Euros.

If you arrive at night, use bus N4, which goes from Plaza Cibeles to Barajas district.

By Bus

Madrid has 8 large intercity and international bus stations. Check the tourist office for info about their destinations. If you are from Barcelona or Bilbao, you can check out buses at Avenida de America bus terminal. Other intercity buses arrive and depart from Estación Sur de Autobuses.

Bus Website

http://www.eurolines.es/en/

By Train

You can use Renfe to and from Madrid: This will get you to either of the two main stations, Atocha and Chamartín both of which have excellent metro connections.

Train Website

http://www.eurail.com/

By Car

If you prefer car travel, you can hire one from such global car rental car companies like Avis, Hertz, Europcar, Budget, and Thrifty.

Moving Around Madrid
Madrid has an excellent public transport system, which is highly recommended. Nonetheless, you can move around the city using five main ways.

Metro (Tube, subway or underground)
The trains work from 06:00 to 01:30. During the day, you won't have to wait for more than five minutes for a train. The trains become slightly scarce from around 19:00, but even then, you won't have to wait for more than thirty minutes.

The metro is a safe, clean and efficient service that's easy to navigate. It has spacious and air conditioned coaches, and many are designed with reserved seating for the disabled and the elderly. The metro is also cheap, with a single ticket going for as little as €1.50. The cheapest alternative is to purchase a ten-journey metro-bus ticket, which costs €12.20 and is applicable on the bus.

Metro Website
https://www.metromadrid.es/en
Phone:902 444 403

Metro & public transport tickets
You can purchase an individual ticket for €1.50 to go anywhere on the metro. This is valid for a single journey on every day of the week, which passes through any zone on the network, and entitles you to an EMT bus journey as well. Metro tickets can be purchased at the automatic ticket machine or the ticket office. The tickets are priced at €1.50 for a single trip anywhere within zone A.

Metro Tickets Website
https://www.metromadrid.es/en/
viaja_en_metro/index.html
Madrid Card Website
http://www.madridcard.com/en/inicio

Note: Madrid's public transport system can be pretty complicated for a foreigner to understand. This is especially because how much you pay will ultimately depend on the line you will use, the specific number of stations, which you want to travel and the specific company that owns that line. Nonetheless, you can get more info about real time public transport system in Madrid by visiting Plan A Metro Madrid to help you understand how public transport works and the different routes. You can also get more from Madrid Tourist Guide to unleash some interesting ideas on how to move around Madrid and end up saving.

Taxi service
Official taxis in Madrid are white with a red stripe.

*Tele taxi: +34 63 090 7990/ +34 91 371 3711/ +34 91 371 2131
*Radio taxi: +34 91 405 5500/ +34 91 405 1213/ +34 91 447 3232/ +34 91 447 5180

You can hire a taxi at night when the metro isn't running, especially if you are not familiar with your surroundings. You can either stop the taxi in the street, or wait for one at a taxi rank. The taxi ranks are shown by a blue sign, containing a white letter T. A green light will be displayed by the available taxis. You will be charged €2.05 for setting the meter, and 98 cents per kilometre after that between 06:00 and 22:00 in the city centre.

If you pick up the cab at Madrid Barajas airport, you will pay an automatic supplement of €5.50. Any trip starting from a taxi rank at railway station, approach road or bus station to either will cost a supplement charge of €2.95. This supplement is mandatory if you take your cab from a taxi zone indicating the sign "supplemento autorizado", which is displayed on a tablet at the taxi rank, reminiscent of a road sign.

Public buses

This is another cheap, clean and efficient means of transport in Madrid, Spain. You can purchase a ten journey Metro-bus ticket for a mere €12.20, which is useable both on the bus and the metro. The EMT buses are painted red, and operate from 06:00 to 23:30. As soon as you get on the bus, simply punch your ticket into the machine. There is a bus service that operates during the night, but if you are not too familiar with your destination, it is advisable to stick to taxis for night travel.

Terminals
*Estación Sur de Madrid: Méndez Álvaro, 83 ;
tel : +34 91 468 4200
Estacion Bus Terminal Map
https://goo.gl/maps/7HuFPHbzPro

*Alsa: Buses travel to all parts of Spain.
Tel: +34 91 327 0540
Alsa Bus Terminal Map
https://goo.gl/maps/uNpdBbmqZJk

*Socibus: Services operate to Jerez de la Frontera, Huelva, Córodoba, Cádiz and Sevilla.
Tel: +34 90 222 9292
Socibus Map

https://goo.gl/maps/beyzz5CRGX72

*Estación de Avenida de América :
Avda. de América, 9 ; Tel : +34 90 230 2010
Estación de Avenida de América Map
https://goo.gl/maps/MzWU4suBeQD2

Travelling within the city on a bus

The buses within the city are red, and are known as EMT, short for Empresa Municipal de Transporte. You can use them to get to any part of the city. They mainly operate on their own bus lanes, helping them avoid traffic most of the time. They operate more or less between 06:00 – 23:30, in relation to the particular line. There are also night buses that run between 23:30 and 05:00, exact times depending on the line. The red bus stops are vividly conspicuous, with each having a timetable attached to it.

The buses at night are referred to as "buhos", meaning "owls". You can usually wait up to half an hour for a bus in the night, but the fare remains the same as during the day.

These buses operate along twenty different routes, and each one must passes through Plaza de la Cibeles. This is especially handy because it is only fifteen minutes away from Sol and Gran Via (the centre), where most of the nightlife is.

A single bus ticket costs €1.50, but if you plan to travel around the city, the best value is probably to purchase a Metro-bus ticket for €12.20 that allows you ten trips on the bus or metro.

Walking around

Madrid's main centre is not really that big, and it's relatively safe to walk around. Majority of the points of interest are indicated on brown pedestrian signs depicting a walking man. If it is not too hot, it can be nice to walk around the city in order to get your bearings better, and capture some beautiful sights along the way.

5

Hotels

Accommodation

There are several types of accommodation in Madrid, with each catering for different types of needs. Hotels are ideal for business people or couples, apartments offer great value and facilities for groups, families or anyone who wants to feel like they are truly experiencing the city. On the other hand, a hostal, which is more like a guesthouse, provides quality accommodation while a youth hostel is ideal for backpackers or anyone on a tight budget.

Budget hotels

These hotels all have 2 stars. You will be charged roughly €60.00 for a twin room.
- ***Asturias**

Tel: +34 91 429 6676
(Calle Sevilla, 2, 28014 Madrid)
This hotel has one hundred and seventy five rooms. It is a central location with clubs, bars, and shops nearby.
Asturias Hotel Website
http://www.hotel-asturias.com/
Asturias Map
https://goo.gl/maps/QL7JjyoppgN2
- ***Mediodia**

Tel: +34 91 527 3060

(Plaza Emperador Carlos V, 8, 28012 Madrid)

This is a big hotel with one hundred and seventy three rooms, and it is close to the Atocha train station and the Reina Sofia Museum.

Mediodia Hotel Website

http://www.mediodiahotel.com/en/

Mediodia Hotel Map

https://goo.gl/maps/sr6848e3qmv

- *Mora

Tel: +34 91 420 1569

(Paseo del Prado, 32, 28014 Madrid)

This hotel has sixty-two rooms, with a convenient distance from Atocha train station, as well as a walking distance to the Reina Sofia Museum.

Mora Hotel Website

http://www.hotelmora.com/index.php/en

Mora Hotel Map

https://goo.gl/maps/PsD8jvQWJ1M2

- *Santander

Tel: +34 91 429 9551

(Calle Echegaray, 1, 28014 Madrid)

This hotel has thirty-five rooms, and is in a central location.

Santander Hotel Website

http://casualhoteles.com/hoteles-madrid/casual-del-teatro/

Santander Hotel Map

https://goo.gl/maps/R61bZKB5dpL2

Hostals

This is similar to a hotel in style, since you pay for both a bathroom and bedroom, but it does not come with the same facilities. It is therefore cheaper than a hotel. You can rent a room with its own bathroom, or one with a shared bathroom. There will be towels and television available, but many do not offer breakfast. Generally, hostels are designed in a modern style and are clean and pleasant places to stay.

- ***Hostal Astoria**

Tel: +34 91 429 1188
(Carrera de San Jerónimo 30-32, 28014 Madrid)
Hostal Astoria Website
http://www.hostal-astoria.com/en/
Hostal Astoria Map
https://goo.gl/maps/2Mxs8NkYUxm

- ***Ostal Gran Duque**

Tel: +34 91 540 0413
(Calle Campomanes, 6 - 3º, 28013 Madrid)
Ostal Gran Duque Website
http://en.granhotelcondeduque.com/
Ostal Gran Duque Map
https://goo.gl/maps/GvrTiBdjQM62

- ***Hostal Don Diego**

Tel: +34 91 521 1339
(Calle Velazquez, 45, 28001 Madrid)
Hostal Don Diego Website
http://www.hostaldondiego.com/en/
Hostal Don Diego Map
https://goo.gl/maps/4JzqCttvuBm

Youth hostels

Do not confuse between a hostal and a youth hostel. A youth hostel, or Albergue Juvenile, has shared sleeping dormitories (typically of the same sex), and sometimes a few group or family rooms for rent. They are one of the most cost effective means of accommodation, and a bed will cost you roughly €15.00 per night. They are a great place to meet other students and travelers, and you will be able to access loads of information from other residents about what is happening in the city.

REAJ, the Youth hostels Network, is responsible for the IYHF in Spain.

- *REAJ

Tel: +34 91 720 1165
Youth Hostels Website
https://www.hihostels.com/

6

Museums

Madrid has more than forty-four museums. Here are a few of the most popular:
- ***The Royal Palace**

Tel: +34 91 454 8800; Street: Bailen

Opened from 10:30 to 6:00pm (Monday to Saturday, October to March); 10:00am to 6:00pm (Sundays and holidays); and 10:00am to 8:00pm (Monday to Sunday, including holidays, April to September)

Entry fee: 10 Euros without a guide; 17 Euros with a guide. Free access for children under five, and 5Euros for pre-arranged visit

This is one of the most visited museums in the city. It was built during the Bourbon reign between the seventeenth and eighteenth centuries. Although the Spanish Royal Family no longer lives here, they still use it for state events. The porcelain room is one of the more unusual rooms, where the walls are covered with white and green porcelain.

Royal Palace Website
http://www.patrimonionacional.es/en
Royal Palace Map
https://goo.gl/maps/KeHJ54CUeJr

- ***Lazaro Galdiano Museum**

Tel: +34 91 561 6084; Street: C/ Serrano, 122
   Opened from 10:00am to 4:30pm (Wednesday to Monday)
   Entry fee: 4 Euros; free on Wednesdays

This museum was originally Jose Lazaro Galdiano's house, who was a financier, editor and writer. He lived between 1862 and 1947, during which time he established an extensive art collection, along several unusual items.

Lazaro Galdiano Website
http://www.flg.es/
Lazaro Galdiano Map
https://goo.gl/maps/qBVmyksEFSr
- ***The Museum of America**

Tel: +34 91 549 2641; Street: Avda. Reyes Catolicos, 6

Opened from 9:30am to 8:30pm Tuesday to Saturday (1st May to 31st October); 9:30am to 6:30pm Tuesday to Saturday (1st November to 30th April); and 10:00am to 3:00pm (Sundays and public holidays)

Entry fee: 3 Euros; free for over 65s and under 18s.

This interesting museum is filled with artifacts from Spain's colonization of the Americas. It covers over two floors, with many pieces preserved since prehistoric times. Here, you will find gold ornaments from Columbia and Mayan parchments from AD 1250.

Museum of America Website
http://www.mecd.gob.es/museodeamerica/en/el-museo.html
Museum of America Map

https://goo.gl/maps/zFazYbakqb62
- *Traje Museum

Tel: +34 91 550 4700
Opened from 9:30am to 7:00pm Tuesday to Saturday; 10:00am to 3:00pm Sundays and Public holidays.

Entry fee: 3 Euros; Free entry with a Madrid Card; as well as Sundays, Saturday afternoons, World Heritage Day (18 April), International Museum Day (18 May), National Fiesta of Spain (12 October) and Constitution Day (6 December)

This museum is all about Spanish clothing from the eighteenth, nineteenth, and twentieth centuries. The rooms house clothing from different eras, as well as temporary exhibitions.

Traje Museum Website
http://museodeltraje.mcu.es/index.jsp?lang=eng
Traje Museum Map
https://goo.gl/maps/VD4A4yav37v
- *Naval Museum

Tel: +34 91 523 8789; Street: Paseo del Prado, 5
Opened from 10:00am to 6:00pm (Tuesday to Sunday);
Closed from 19th July to 1st September (summer).
Entry: free

Here you will find replicas of the Spanish Navy arsenal from the eighteenth century. The history of the navy is illustrated through charts, weapons, and paintings. Each room shows a different period in history, starting with the fifteenth century to the present day.

Naval Museum Website

http://www.armada.mde.es/ArmadaPortal/page/
Portal/ArmadaEspannola/ciencia_museo/prefLang_en/
Naval Museum Map
https://goo.gl/maps/LaJ7uZcNocF2
- ***Real Madrid Stadium**

Tel: +34 91 453 2902; St: Pº de la Castellana, 144,
Estadio Santiago Bernabéu, Puerta 3
Opened from 10:00am to 7:30pm Monday to Saturday (Days with no matches); and 10:30am to 6:30pm Sundays
Entry fee: Under fourteen – 11 Euros; Adults – 16 Euros

You can visit the Real Madrid Museum when touring the stadium. The museum is broad and full of trophies that date back over the entire history of the teams. In addition, there is a wall of photographs of all the Real Madrid Players to have ever existed, as well as autographed boots and shirts from the first team.

Real Madrid Stadium Website
http://www.realmadrid.com/en/santiago-bernabeu-stadium
Real Madrid Stadium Map
https://goo.gl/maps/eowdGVACPGN2

Extra Time In Madrid
Other notable museums worth visiting include:
- **Museum Cerralbo**

Museum Cerralbo Website
http://en.museocerralbo.mcu.es/
Museum Cerralbo Map
https://goo.gl/maps/FmRWa2rJk5B2

· National Archaeological Museum of Spain

National Archaeological Website
http://www.man.es/man/en/home
National Archaeological Map
https://goo.gl/maps/5C3dohU34uR2

7

Art Galleries

- ***The Prado**

Prado Art Gallery, Tel: +34 91 330 2800; Street: Paseo Del Prado
Opened from Tuesday to Sunday (9:00am to 8:00pm)
€12.00 entry fee; free entry for official guides, teachers, disabled, unemployed EU students below age 25, and over 65s

This is probably the most famous art gallery in Madrid. It accommodates a wide collection of works from the twelfth to the nineteenth centuries. Here, you will see some of the most talked about paintings in the world, including works by Murillo, Rubens, and Goya.

Prado Website
https://www.museodelprado.es/en/
Prado Map
https://goo.gl/maps/uPk4h7zDXWJ2
- ***Reina Sofia**

Reina Sofia Art Gallery; Tel: +34 91 774 1000; street: Santa Isabel, 52
Opened from 10:00am to 9:00pm (Monday to Saturday), and 10:00am to 2:30pm on Sundays.

Entry fee: 6 Euros; free for the general public from 2:30pm to 9:30pm

Saturdays, 10:00am to 2:30pm Sundays, and on 6th December, 12th October and 18th May.

This is an impressive art gallery where you can see relatively recent works from the twentieth and twenty-first centuries. There are several Picasso pieces, including the popular Guernica, and a separate section designated for some modern art sculptures, as well as a room showing a film written by Salvador Dali and Bunuel.

Reina Sofia Website
http://www.museoreinasofia.es/en
Reina Sofia Map
https://goo.gl/maps/Dk7DHHhb6V62
- *Thyssen Bornemisza

Thyssen Bornemisza Art Gallery; Tel: +34 91 369 0151; Street: Paseo del Prado, 8
Open from 10:00am to 7:00pm (Tuesday to Sunday)
Entry fee: 8 Euros for adults; 5:50 Euros for students and pensioners; free for children under twelve (accompanied)

This is one of the most popular art galleries, and the main building is known as Villahermosa Palace. The paintings here are said to be among the best private collections from the thirteenth to the twentieth century art. Here, you will see Rothko, Kandinsky, Renoir, Degas, Goya, Titian or Durero. There are guided tours for families with children aged between six and twelve years at the weekends. You must call to book in advance.

Thyssen Bornemisza Website
http://www.museothyssen.org/en/thyssen/home
Thyssen Bornemisza Map
https://goo.gl/maps/gPRVwPUcrg32

- ***Sorolla Art Gallery**

Tel: +34 91 310 1584; Street: del General Martínez Campos, 37
 Opened from 9:30 am to 8:00pm (Tuesday to Saturday); and 10:00am to 3:00pm (Sundays and public holidays)
 Entry fee: 3 Euros for Adults; free for pensioners and students, and on Sundays.

This is a less publicized museum, but one of the little known treasures in Madrid. The art gallery was originally inhabited by Joaquin Sorolla y Bastida, the Valencian artist. It was built from 1910 to 1911. Here, you will find excellent ceramic works and sculptures, as well as jewelry and furniture.

Sorolla Website
http://museosorolla.mcu.es/
Sorolla Map
https://goo.gl/maps/tWEXD46bof62

8

Shopping In Madrid

Shopping in Madrid is so much fun because there are very many different styles to select from. The prices are fairly reasonable, unless you are shopping in designer boutiques.

There are 5 areas you should head off too if you are looking to shop in Madrid: Cuatro Caminos, Princesa, Chueca and Salamanca. Each area serves different budgets and tastes.

Chueca is a popular bohemian area where you can find designer and original goods, with price tags to match. Calle Hortaleza is one of the best streets to visit. Chueca is particularly good for shoe shopping. It's not far from the center, and you can walk to the area in five minutes if you are in Gran Via.

Chueca Map
https://goo.gl/maps/rUW5AfjyDdK2

Shopping in the center of the city is a delight. The most obvious areas to visit are the Puerta del Sol, Gran Via, Plaza Mayor and the nearby streets. You will find Spanish high street names such as El Corte Ingles, Fnac, Bershka, Pimkie and Zara.

Puerta del Sol Map
https://goo.gl/maps/G9tyXVdfK8N2
Gran Via Map
https://goo.gl/maps/YLTKXDzcAx32
Plaza Mayor Map
https://goo.gl/maps/51i1YC7SNAS2

If you are working on a budget, consider shopping close to the university in Arguelles. Begin your shopping on the streets of Alberto Aguilera and Princesa. Cuatro Caminos, located in the north of the city, is another great bargain paradise. It is located between the streets of Orense and Bravo Murillo, close to Plaza de Castilla.

Arguelles Map
https://goo.gl/maps/JUnvt3MG4Ww
Cuatro Caminos Map

https://goo.gl/maps/aNYL4co5yjt

9

Dining In Madrid

Dining In Madrid

Madrid has the richest variety of cuisine in Spain. Its public eating spots cover everything, including Andalusian gazpacho, Valencian paella, Galician pulpo (octopus), Basque bacalao (cod), and Asturian fabada (strong pork stew). You will also find Madrid's very own lamb and vegetable stew (cocido), tripe (callos), and the lesser popular oreja (ears).

The dishes in the region are both logical and hearty, given the winter climate and setting, but the most interesting thing is that the city is actually landlocked. It is surrounded by a large arid plateau, and receives a daily fish supply that is transported through large containers from the Atlantic north to supply top restaurants such as Cabo Mayor and La Trainera, with the best and freshest seafood in the country.

Meals
*Breakfast: Breakfast is typically tea, hot chocolate or coffee, with assorted rolls, jam and butter. Spanish breakfast might also include churros, which are thin, fried doughnuts, or porras (which are basically bigger churros).

*Lunch: This is the most important meal of the day in the country, and is reminiscent to the midday, farm style dinner in the U.S. It usually includes 3 or 4 courses, starting with an option of soup or a variety of dishes of hors d'oeuvres known as entremeses. Usually, a dish of egg or fish is served after this, followed by a meat dish with vegetables. Wine is always included in the meal. Dessert is typically assorted fruit, custard, or pastry, followed by coffee. Lunchtime starts from 1:00 to 4:00 pm, with rush hour being at 2:00 pm.

*Tapas: Once they are done with their early evening strolls, most Spaniards head to their favourite bars, tascas where they drink wine and bite assorted tapas (snacks), like olives, eggs in mayonnaise, or bits of fish.

Since most Spaniards take their dinner very late, they usually eat an extremely light breakfast, mostly coffee and maybe a pastry. But they often get hungry by 11:00 am, and since lunch might not be ready until 1:00 pm, they usually take a late morning snack at a cafeteria. Most preferred items to order include an empanada (slice of fish or meat pie from Galicia) or tortilla (omelette with potatoes) accompanied with a caña of beer or a copa of wine. Enquire for a doble if you want a larger beer. Many people ask for a large tapa, like squid (calamares), or tripe (callos), also served with wine or beer and bread.

*Dinner: A typical meal begins with a bowl of soup, with the second course usually being a fish dish, and a third main course, usually pork, beef, or veal, served with vegetables. Again, desserts are often pastries, custard, or fruit.

If you had a late and heavy lunch and stopped at a tapas bar before dinner, supper will automatically be much lighter, perhaps a bowl of soup, sausage, some cold cuts, or a Spanish omelet with potatoes. Wine is always included in the meal. Typically, dining usually begins at 10:00 or 10:30pm.

Where to eat
- **Alkalde**

Address: Calle de Jorge Juan, 10, Madrid
Phone: +34 915 76 33 59
Alkalde Website
http://www.alkalderestaurante.com/
Alkalde Map
https://goo.gl/maps/WFUwfE7btYD2
- **Bazaar Restaurant**

Address: Calle de la Libertad, 21, Madrid
Phone: +34 915 23 39 05

Bazaar Website
http://www.grupandilana.com/es/restaurantes/bazaar
Bazaar Map
https://goo.gl/maps/oScyUCWuFG32

- **Sobrino de Botin**

This is the world oldest Restaurant; they serve traditional Spanish food from different regions.

Address: Calle Cuchilleros, 17, 28005 Madrid
Phone: +34 913 66 42 17
Sobrino de Botin Website
http://www.botin.es/?q=en
Sobrino de Botin Map
https://goo.gl/maps/xu31t8TD6tv

- **Ribeira do Mino**

Try some amazing Galician seafood Ribeira do Mino.

Address: Calle de Sta Brigida, 1, Madrid
Phone: +34 915 21 98 54
Ribeira do Mino Website
http://www.marisqueriaribeiradomino.com/en/des-752-home
Ribeira do Mino Map
https://goo.gl/maps/ATeDHDJ1BNs

- **Paella de la Reina**

Eat some of the best Valencian paella at Paella de la Reina.

Address: Calle de la Reina, 39, 28004 Madrid
Phone: +34 915 31 18 85
Paella de la Reina
http://www.lapaelladelareina.com/
Paella de la Reina
https://goo.gl/maps/G3K5bnu9i1w

10

Bars And Nightlife

MADRID

Madrid loves to party. With near-compulsory siestas after lunch and sometimes in the evening as well, who can blame the three million inhabitants of this great city for wanting to burn off all the excess energy? Despite its flair and cultural sophistication, Madrid's vibrant nightlife and unpretentious bar scene provide endless opportunities to do just that. At a time when most tourists from the more sensible parts of the world might be settling into a pair of slippers and warm cocoa, Madrileños are just getting started. If you have the urge and liveliness to join them, here is a quick sample of what is on offer in Madrid after dark.

8:00pm: Tapas, canas and friends
Going out in Madrid usually starts with a relaxing after work drink that soon turns into a frantic adventure, rarely ending before 2:00 am. Some of the reasons behind the late schedule include the exceptionally strong cocktails, a rather laid-back attitude on when and where to meet, and the utter volume of venues from which to choose from.

However, once you have committed yourself to going out, it is probably best to give up any other plans for the evening and simply enjoy the ride. Unlike many nightlife scenes, what you wear is not particularly significant – it is not unusual to see a posh individual (a well dressed pijo) interacting with a T-shirt sporting twenty-something. The best locations to soak up the local ambiance are the areas of La Latina, Malasana and Plaza de Santa Ana, which are ever bustling, particularly at night. Most young people (and not-so-young individuals) gather at one of the many tapas bars to enjoy cold beers (canas) with an array of tapas. But be warned – many tapas bars are small and tend to get overcrowded with standing room only.
- *Lateral, Paseo de La Castellana

Open from 8:00am to 1:00am (Monday to Wednesday); 8:00am to 2:00am (Thursday and Friday); 12:00pm to 2:00 am (Saturday) and 12:00pm to 1:00 am (Sunday).

Phone: +34 914 20 15 82
Lateral Website
http://www.lateral.com/
Lateral Map
https://goo.gl/maps/8zRb8JBJLxF2

- *Le Cabrera, Calle de Dona Barbara de Braganza 2

Open from 4:00pm to 2:00 am (Monday to Thursday); 4:00pm to 2:30am (Friday and Saturday); and from 1:30pm (Sunday brunch).
Standouts include an impressive collection of cocktails starting from €11 and the foie gras topped burgers.

Phone: +34 913 19 94 57
Le Cabrera Website
http://www.cienllaves.com/terraza/
Le Cabrera Map
https://goo.gl/maps/r5CpB3fBkKG2

10:00pm – Copas

If you are not satisfied with tapas, it is good to know that 10:00 pm is the earliest time Madrileños venture out to dinner, and most restaurants account for this schedule. Some people remain at the bars and order larger raciones, while others, recuperating from their evening siestas, are rejuvenated and ready for the night's revelries. After the evening meal, it is usually time to enjoy some cocktails or copas, as opposed to wine.

- *Bristol Bar, Calle del Almirante 20

BARS AND NIGHTLIFE

Open from 10:00 am to 1:00 am (Monday to Wednesday); 10:00 am to 2:00am (Thursday and Friday); 11:00am to 2:00am (Saturday)

During summertime, it is standard to hop from one terrace venue to the next between 2:00am and 3:00am. When it gets colder, folks usually stay at their favorite bars until it is time to venture into the clubs. It is usually challenging to keep up with changing trends in a city as cosmopolitan as this, but locals still remain obsessed with the classic tonic and gin. Tours, tastings and entire bars are designated for the timeless combination, like the Brit-motivated Bristol Bar.

Phone: +34 915 22 45 68
Bristol Bar Website
http://bristolbar.es/
Bristol Bar Map
https://goo.gl/maps/JwENRf69g2v
- ***Ramses, Plaza de la Independencia**

Open from 11:00am to 2:30 am every day

Interior design enthusiasts love the Philippe Starck décor at this ultra chic bar and restaurant.

Phone:+34 914 35 16 66
Ramses Website
http://www.ramseslife.com/
Ramses Map
https://goo.gl/maps/9iWfGDG1Y6o
- ***Museo Chicote, Gran Via 12**

Open from 5:00pm to 3:00am (Sunday to Thursday); 5:00pm to 3:30am (Friday and Saturday)

If you are up for a sense of nostalgia, you might love this art deco bar that has hosted luminaries such as Hemingway, Gardner, and Sinatra since its establishment in 1931.

Phone:+34 915 32 67 37
Museo Chicote Website
http://grupomercadodelareina.com/en/museo-chicote-en/
Museo Chicote Map
https://goo.gl/maps/dbmfnA26K842

3:00am: Nightclubs

When the bars close up, the diehards continue partying at the many nightclubs in the city. Most are opened at midnight but only start swinging after 1:30am. For the clubs that stay open until 6:00am at the very least, things don't generally heat up until 4:00am.

- *Joy Eslava, Calle Arsenal 11

Open from 11:30 pm every day

The constant factor is the collective energy that fuels the legendary nightlife of Madrid long after the majority of cities have hit the sack. The dance floor at Joy Eslava is enormous, the crowd is mixed, and the décor is slightly dated. However, with a low cover charge, inventive club nights, and surprise appearances from ostentatious dancers, it offers kitschy, harmless fun until 6:00am.

Phone:+34 913 66 54 39
Joy Eslava Website
http://joy-eslava.com/Joy_Madrid/Bienvenida.html
Joy Eslava Map
https://goo.gl/maps/n8ZPJpDJ2GJ2

- *Gabana 1800, Calle Velazquez 6

Open from 12:00am to 5:00am (Wednesday to Sunday)

As you might expect, there is a VIP tables galore, a velvet rope, and an impressive list of celebrity visitors. It has a strict door policy, so hopefuls come early.

Phone:+34 915 75 18 46
Gabana Website
http://www.gabana.es/
Gabana Map
https://goo.gl/maps/VTMgFrwmWM52

11

Special Things To Do While In Madrid

Eat at Botin: This is the world's oldest restaurant and has featured in the Guinness Book of Records.

Botin Website
http://www.botin.es/?q=en

Botin Map
https://goo.gl/maps/Hdr7sL2Aa8T2

Watch Real Madrid Playing: If you love football, Real Madrid Football Club has many of the world's best football players. Watching them play live from their home stadium, Santiago Bernabeu Stadium, will definitely be an experience you will never forget.

Real Madrid Website
http://www.realmadrid.com/en/santiago-bernabeu-stadium
Real Madrid Map
https://goo.gl/maps/fmymBPxSgqu

Watch Flamenco: Madrid prides in having some of the world's finest flamenco dancers.

Flamenco Website
http://www.flamencotickets.com/madrid-flamenco-shows

Shop at the El Rastro: This weekly flea market has literally anything you can think of so visiting it to buy a few souvenirs won't be such a bad idea. This is the largest flea market in Europe.

Address: Calle Ribera de Curtidores
Phone:+34 915 29 82 10
El Rastro Map
https://goo.gl/maps/Qb4h4cGgdnG2

Watch bullfighting in Ventas Bullring: Madrid has some of the best bullfighters in Spain so schedule to attend one of the fixtures. You can learn more about bullfighting in Madrid here.

Address: Plaza del Carmen 1
Phone: +34 915 319 131
Bullfighting Website
https://www.bullfightticketsmadrid.com/en/home

Try riding on Madrid's cable car: Riding the famously called teleferico will definitely give you breathtaking views of Madrid as you tour different attraction sites.

Address: Paseo del Pintor Rosales
Phone: +34 902 34 50 02
Teleferico Website
http://teleferico.com/
Teleferico Map

SPECIAL THINGS TO DO WHILE IN MADRID

Try exploring Madrid's green places: One of its very famous is Casa de Campo, which is five times bigger than New York's Central Park. You can also check out El Retiro Park where you can hire a rowboat or even check out the statute of the Fallen Angel.

Address: Paseo Puerta del Angel, 1
Casa de Campo Map
https://goo.gl/maps/fi1KMaQoBQy

Address: Plaza de la Independencia, 7
Phone: +34 915 30 00 41
El Retiro Park Map
https://goo.gl/maps/Ce7xEPboBtS2

Try the famous chocolate con churros: These are really tasty sticks of fried dough eaten by just dunking in a mug of warm dipping chocolate. It tastes more like the Spanish biscuits and tea.

Address: Pasadizo San Ginés, 5
Phone: +34 913 65 65 46
Con Churros Website
https://chocolateriasangines.com/
Con Churros Map
https://goo.gl/maps/UnEzGCb2hvG2

See the spectacular city gate Puerto de Alcala: This is especially amazing at night. It was constructed by Francesco Sabatini for King Charles III. You can learn more about it here.

Address: Plaza de la Independencia, 1
Puerto de Alcala Map
https://goo.gl/maps/tYhZnyzPCVo

See the Golden Triangle: This one is formed by the city's 3 main museums, Reina Sofia Museum, Thyssen Boremisza and Prado Museum.

Reina Sofia Museum Map
https://goo.gl/maps/RUayEfC4k5T2
Thyssen Boremisza Map
https://goo.gl/maps/YMkhtUhYWvS2
Prado Museum Map
https://goo.gl/maps/gwh8XjD8nHM2

Visit the Temple of Debod: This is definitely one of the unusual places to see in Parque del Oeste; this is a park just near the Royal Palace. You can learn more about it here.

Temple of Debod Map
https://goo.gl/maps/ogfqNQV7Krr

12

Three Day Sample Itinerary

Three Day Sample Itinerary

Madrid is an astonishingly easy city to get around, be it by public transportation or by foot. Do not stress about tipping; a few coins for meal service will usually be enough. Generally, wait-staff are not awfully attentive: If you want to ask for the bill or place an order, you can simply flag down any waiter. While the city is relatively safe, there is plenty of petty theft. Always mind your belongings because pickpockets do not discriminate against tourists.

Day One

- *Royal Palace of Madrid

This is the place to experience Spanish richness at its best. The rooms are a genuine wonderland of red velvet thrones, crystal chandeliers, and ceiling murals galore.

While you are there, visit the Almudena Cathedral in the neighborhood. Entrance is free, but a small donation is still welcomed. Plan to stay for one to two hours.

Address: Calle de Bailén, 3

Phone: +34 914 54 87 00
Royal Palace Map
https://goo.gl/maps/RWFxNaY7ViQ2
- ***Plaza Mayor**

Surround yourself with Madrid culture in the main square of the capital, Plaza Mayor. On summer, it floods with outdoor terrazas where tourists and locals alike drink and dine al fresco. During winter, it is covered with an array of lights that highlights the yearly Christmas fair.

Plaza Mayor houses some of the most classic gift shops, where you can acquire traditional Spanish souvenirs, including thimbles and hats. It is usually filled with street performers and real-sized cartoon characters. Plan to stay for less than an hour.

Plaza Mayor Map
https://goo.gl/maps/f6tz89J9M9s
- ***Puerta del Sol**

This is the most classic meeting point in the city. Many bus and metro lines pass through here, and all the radial freeways in the country are measured from a little plaque in the square. Puerta del Sol also hosts one of the biggest events of the year: New Year's Eve. The locals celebrate by quickly eating twelve grapes in a row, and in tune with the strikes of the clock.

If you are hungry, you can grab something sweet to eat at the La Mallorquina bakery, which is over a century old. Plan to stay for less than an hour.

Puerta del Sol Map
https://goo.gl/maps/3254KMhcnCw
- ***La Latina**

Experience the best tapas hopping culture in Madrid by visiting La Latina, a tapas bar-filled neighborhood. If you happen to be in Madrid on Sunday, be sure to pass by the neighboring El Rastro outdoor market. Plan to stay for two to three hours.

La Latina Map
https://goo.gl/maps/znWJhbs7JY32

Day Two
- *Gran Via

This is the busiest street in Madrid, and arguably the most attractive thoroughfare. It is also where you can find a heavy concentration of internationally known stores and theaters. Go there to shop, see a show, or just wonder at the buzz of the big city. Plan to stay for less than an hour.

Gran Via Map
https://goo.gl/maps/jkoC78c4pVE2
- **Plaza de Cibeles**

There is probably no panorama more charming than the Plaza de Cibeles, with the grand Cibeles Palace and the chariot topped fountain. The H.Q. of the Spanish postal service was once based in the Cibeles Palace, but it is now home to the City Hall and a cultural center known as CentroCentro. Plan to stay for less than an hour.

Plaza de Cibeles Map
https://goo.gl/maps/CAwHnfQwGfC2
- **Retiro Park (Parque del Retiro)**

This is where all the city clickers in Spain go to get a dose of fresh air. Go there to row a boat, take a stroll, or sit back and enjoy a beverage at one of the several outdoor cafes. If you are a museum or art buff, and have some time to spare, visit the neighboring Prado Museum that is home to some of the finest artwork in Europe. The Glass Palace or Palacio de Cristal is free to enter and usually hosts fascinating installations and art exhibitions. Plan to stay for one to two hours.

Retiro Park Map
https://goo.gl/maps/mHW7fqWGp4C2
- ***Barrio de Salamanca**

This neighborhood is famous for its specially posh residents, as well as the fancy restaurants and shops that they frequent. Plan to stay for one to two hours.

Barrio de Salamanca Map
https://goo.gl/maps/LuzhVfaM5892

Day Three
- *San Anton Market

Recently renovated, this is a new hotspot for gastro lovers, especially because it is one part old fashioned, complete with fish, produce and meat stands, and the other part modern connoisseur paradise, including tapas bars and a rooftop bar & restaurant. Plan to stay for one to two hours.

Address: Calle de Augusto Figueroa, 24B
Phone: +34 913 30 07 30
San Anton Market Map
https://goo.gl/maps/afqPRqYhYAB2
- *Plaza del Dos de Mayo

This is the heart and soul of the city's diverse Malasana neighborhood, and the location of numerous outdoor terrazos, playgrounds, and often even flea markets and fairs. This is the perfect place to grab a tinto de verano or cana as you mix with the locals and just watch. In the side streets of the neighborhood, you will discover funky shops, cafes, and restaurants. Plan to stay for one to two hours.

Plaza del Dos de Mayo Map
https://goo.gl/maps/Kaq734p5XB52
- *Antigua Casa Crespo

Spanish souvenirs do not get more legit than a pair of espadrilles (alpargatas) from this family run establishment that is over a century year old. The shoes are completely Spanish made, and very affordable, with a pair going for under ten Euros. The service is also phenomenal, and the scenery will make you feel like you are going back in time. Plan to stay for less than an hour.

Address: Calle del Divino Pastor, 29
Phone: +34 915 21 56 54
Antigua Casa Crespo Website
https://www.antiguacasacrespo.com/password
Antigua Casa Crespo Map

- *Bodega de la Ardosa

As far as Spanish bars are concerned, this is about as classic as it gets. Think shelves piled with dusty wine bottles, colorfully tiled walls, and memorabilia from the establishment's 100 years+ in business. The best part is their addictively tasty tortilla Espanola, notoriously considered to be one of the best in the city. Plan to stay for less than an hour.

Address: Calle de Colón, 13
Phone:+34 915 21 49 79
Bodega de la Ardosa Website
http://www.laardosa.es/
Bodega de la Ardosa Map
https://goo.gl/maps/qntravw46eu

13

Conclusion

I want to thank you for reading this book! I sincerely hope that you received value from it!

Ó Copyright 2016 by Gary Jones - All rights reserved.

This document is geared towards providing exact and reliable information in regards to the topic and issue covered. The publication is sold with the idea that the publisher is not required to render accounting, officially permitted, or otherwise, qualified services. If advice is necessary, legal or professional, a practiced individual in the profession should be ordered.

- From a Declaration of Principles which was accepted and approved equally by a Committee of the American Bar Association and a Committee of Publishers and Associations.

In no way is it legal to reproduce, duplicate, or transmit any part of this document in either electronic means or in printed format. Recording of this publication is strictly prohibited and any storage of this document is not allowed unless with written permission from the publisher. All rights reserved.

The information provided herein is stated to be truthful and consistent, in that any liability, in terms of inattention or otherwise, by any usage or abuse of any policies, processes, or directions contained within is the solitary and utter responsibility of the recipient reader.

Under no circumstances will any legal responsibility or blame be held against the publisher for any reparation, damages, or monetary loss due to the information herein, either directly or indirectly.

Respective authors own all copyrights not held by the publisher.

The information herein is offered for informational purposes solely, and is universal as so. The presentation of the information is without contract or any type of guarantee assurance.

The trademarks that are used are without any consent, and the publication of the trademark is without permission or backing by the trademark owner. All trademarks and brands within this book are for clarifying purposes only and are the owned by the owners themselves, not affiliated with this document.

Printed in Great Britain
by Amazon